Corrina Bain

Debridement

weather
for

Printed in the United States of America

First Edition
ISBN: 978-0-9857317-5-5
Library of Congress Control Number: 2015935400

Book design: Jane Ormerod
Cover photograph: Gina Williams
Photograph of Corrina Bain: Syreeta McFadden
Editors: Jane Ormerod, Thomas Fucaloro, David Lawton

great weather for MEDIA, LLC
New York, NY

www.greatweatherformedia.com

Grateful acknowledgement is made to the editors of the following publications in which these works, or earlier versions of them, previously appeared: Villanelles (Everyman's Library Pocket Poets), kill author, Booth, The Rumpus, Union Station.

The death, then, of a beautiful woman is, unquestionably,
the most poetical topic in the world.

—Edgar Allen Poe

Contents

Debridement

Sorry

Her withered breasts. The empty wallet. The Christmas tree ornament's mirrored heart. The shredded roadside tire. Dusky spot on the goldenrod carpet. Metal spike from the train tracks. Black twitching stem of the butterfly without wings. The belt that was a gift. The compact mirror decorated with stickers. Like a make-up case. Like a big girl. Pieces of burnt paper in a drinking glass. Bottles of saline. Bottles of alcohol. Gray fabric sagging from the roof of the minivan. Glass ashtray split through its bottle green middle. The promise. How I knew, even then.

Why I've Done It

Again and again my lover becomes
the deadgirl in my arms.

I turn them towards me on the mattress
and suddenly, they've gone quiet. Their veins blue

as strangled birds. I try to hide the body. Drag it to
the carniceria. To the sidewalk on trash day.

The first few times it happened, I thought
it was something wrong with them. That they'd

been born as dead girls.
That they'd been dead all their lives.

But after the third and fourth
and thirty-seventh time, I realized.

On worse days, I am the dead one.
I open the door for the men and they come in like wind.

No peace. No suture. Bits of skin adhered to the bandage.
The things I want most dreadfully are always

wrong: Her face turning like a lathe against me,
carving me out: Conjured passion

which does not teach: Snared songless
on a tarred string. When X says turn it off,

turn it off. When Z says she just wants to die, I know
what is coming due. The body's costs. Glut of clear fluid,

Milk of the stopped wound. The corpse, coming in.
Saying *Hello.*

First Time

I tried to take it. Not a real
Barbie
a figurine
from a happy meal
smaller
one fused piece.
It was not mine, but so pretty
I thought I needed it. She
belonged to some girl
my parents thought
I should be friends
with but I did
not see
her. The girl had red ears
and light brown hair.
I had eyes only
for the tiny, mute princess. Ballgown
rigid opalescent plastic, deep
pink with light
pink bows. I wanted to
own it.
A picky child, my list of beautiful things was
short: My mother
Baryshnikov
white flowers
some birds
but not all
the doll's pale yellow hair
like a cartoon sun. I shoved her down
my pants. Bulge
in my Levis, imagined what my
innocent face would have

looked like, tried
to copy it. Found out, I cried, claimed
I only meant to borrow it.
Everyone forgave
the obvious lie.
I meant to have her. To measure
and study. Her small
peach-colored neck. To glean
the lesson my parents refused
to teach me, what a
girl is supposed
to be. Then, with
the big rocks
in the yard, to crack her
open.
To find out
how thick the
skin, how thin.
What she was made
of, underneath.

Origin

Your first loves were Styrofoam
wig stands. Mannequin arms. Giant candles
heat-warped into shapes like breasts.
They cluttered the quarry
behind your house. Broken-necked swans
refusing to rot. You said
you tried *to do them right—*
twist of melon-colored nylon lace around
the neck.

You found me and I thought
I had found you. I make many errors
of recognition. Nightbirds for true ghosts. For a long time
I thought the pale things strewn behind you
were parts of women. Hadn't noticed the artifice.

Remember when we met, you were so thin,
it was recognizable. Your heritage. The knife.
Remember when we met
the wild hope we entertained
that you could make me
into something else.

Quotes from the Deadgirl Reality Show Pilot

The Producers Issue a Statement

The nice thing about the genre is that
it is less stylized.
Achievable. Here is
our vision: Dignity.
Knowledge that they
are just like us.
It's entertainment.
The fountain in the front room
like a dream of breath.

The Girls in the Honesty Closet

The fountain? They had to have some gimmick.
The pearl-colored gates are tacky, but at least
they didn't try to make it look like hell.

There was the time Celeste kept the rubber cement
in her room and no one knew where it was.
That was messed up. I needed that.

The flowers on the porch
like a dream of breath
piling up at the door with fan mail.
We are so popular. There's no way to
do us more wrong than we've
been done. No way
to disappoint us.

We won't send them to the store
for tampons. We won't try
to have their baby.
Our moods are dark but constant.

That bitch Shelley keeps wearing my bathrobe.

Outtakes and Deleted Scenes

Mandy with the shotgun hole
in her stomach has her alive-boyfriend
stick his whole hand in there
until he grunts like an ox.

the producers try to force
some tension in the house
because it makes for better television.
Left to themselves, the girls would probably
be friends. Shelley apologizes.

The highlights
in their hair keep turning
brittle, falling out. The group
begins to question the contracts:

You want us to fight
about who should clean the microwave?

My husband turned himself in
with my severed breast oozing in his
coat pocket.

That isn't enough?
Why is there a camera
in the shower?

Sonnet Self-Erasure

the white sliding door of the van

some have the vision to know

every inch of inviolate flesh
            a   canvas
ready to unbirth the bullet

            tight pink shirt
      Angel in   glitterscript

            shapes of the body become
more lovely
                        as I run
                                    wedding cake

packing tape

             tidbits they never found

The Ugliest Woman in the World

was a stage name for
the ringmaster's wife—blackly furred
double row of teeth forcing the lips
out, also called Ape Woman

unclear how old she was when he
bought her her figure *delicate* *stunted*

when the husband lost his main act
in childbirth blood pulled mercilessly
into the world the newborn dead too (documentation
of its fur but not its sex)
he had them preserved
the best taxidermy the time allowed
married another woman with the same
odd gene *hirsute* *bestial*
a bigger spectacle
living bride-exhibit alongside the dead
he began to get rich
the live freak
was amusing but the other was proof

women and men beasts
the gaff of it the grift

a museum
of stolen things would have our best artifacts
many of them bodies

Stage show
where combine the ones who strive
toward freakishness
and the ones who can live their lives as nothing else

we will see this again
pornographer producer
coupled to the living fact of his invention
the choreography conjuring a woman
to fill it

laying ourselves at the feet
of the man prancing around our own corpse

in my time a girl folded beneath the
pearl white doubling
of her cheeks camera auditioning
for the role of gun
in my time replicable beauty
stamped a relentless alabaster identical frame after
frame
the almost-same almost-woman
listing turn-ons favorite music
I too have been the arrangement
lens bulb sex bleaching
my bones into order
airbrush photo shop
what drives us to it
Ugliest Woman in the World
the beast we know we are
furred waist cinched in pink satin
delicate shoes on animal feet breast in a robe of
hair
his tongue shoved in our mouth
like Lucifer enthroned in hell.

True Hollywood Confessions of 1932

My family wanted more for me
than this. The blonde best friend
in a smart little hat.
Vocal training to chirp
an anthology of Yes.
The saddest thing about suicides—
we're not talentless.
The press thought well of me

even when I was in awful shows.
The first attempt, back in Brooklyn.
Some young man had stopped calling
I tried to let it out through the wrists
but it would not go.

I woke up in the cardboard bed,
muslin curtain of minor fame drawn around me,
when they gave my body back to me,
it was nothing I wanted.

Everyone said the stage was dying,
that pictures were the thing
so I came west.

I went up there not planning anything,
a view of the city through the tall letters.
There was a ladder, leaning against the H
like someone knew I was coming—

Soft pacific sky like cotton balls
soaked in foundation, streaking the horizon.
The End in flowing script. I deserved

a starring role, not this
lurid sliver of history: the first
who thought to jump from here.

They'll have to put up fences.
I'm not sorry I came.
I would rather this a thousand times
than be the beauty of some small town.

My family thought the flashbulbs
had been the enemy

now they'll take me back,
empty me out
a champagne flute full of smoke
over the Ohio.

Just as I feared—
the belle of some small place.

How the Corpse Was Known

I came into all this assuming you'd just treat me the way I wanted without ever having to explain what I needed. This time, I won't be so vague.
–Ryan Jenkins in an email to Jasmine Fiore, weeks before her murder.

Surprisingly, your given name. Fragrance too thick
in the air,
your teeth and fingers stolen, proof he'd planned.
The police carried you somewhere clean, cold, the
breasts' architecture undone in the stadium light.

Your teeth and fingers, stolen. Proof he'd planned
to have you laid open, your body's lies untold,
breasts' architecture undone in the stadium light—
he'd loved that part of you, it brought him in

to have you. Laid open, your body's lies untold—
sapphire contacts still blazing in your eyes.
He'd loved that. Part of you, it brought him in
to the *Person of Interest* file, oily gleam of his
showman chest.

Sapphire contacts still blazing in your eyes,
your body folded into the hot, dark suitcase.
In the Person of Interest file, oily gleam of his
showman chest
begging to be believed in, identified.

Your body, folded into the hot, dark suitcase,
clear bags of silicone, their serial numbers
begging to be believed in, identified.
Tanned whip he thought was his to ruin.

Clear bags of silicone, their serial numbers
naming him the one, thief of your breath,
tanned whip he thought was his to ruin.
Terrible heat of the season, Jasmine.

Naming him, the one, thief of your breath
The police carried you somewhere. Clean, cold. The
terrible heat of the season. Jasmine
surprisingly, your given name. Fragrance too thick
        in the air.

Dating Profile

My body haunted and in alarm—
each chewed-through blossom, hum and lull
of destroying insects, disassembling.
Eventually the cunt stops being what it is,
pomegranate thumbed to a mess of seeds.
Food of the land of the dead.

I was born an inkwell spilled
across my mother's red dress.
I was born my father a forgery so good
the museum took the original down.
I was born. I could open you like that

finger by finger into illumination.

C _ _ _ _ _ _ _ _ _ T

AFTER YOUR DEATH

It's been a long time.
I look different.
So do you. Are you
awake in there?
Have you met the girls
again? Did you see
the news story about
you? Flirting with a
transsexual prostitute
bragging about your
physique. The newscaster
wonders if that
makes you gay. Her
lipstick red and wet.

After several people
had your same idea
Craigslist's grimly un-aesthetic face
now asks for my phone number
calls back and offers a code.

It does this only for ads
of a certain suspicious type.
Casual Encounters
asking for the phone
to ring. A man's voice
to threaten me
with sex. Frustrate.
Howling. Because

my voice still sounds
like a girl's. Sunk, husky,
but feminine, apologetic
tilted up
at the end.

I started injections
depo testosterone,
the opposite
of the hormone they use
to chemically castrate
unrepentant sex offenders.
The libido
might be a side effect

I have finally found, in the needle,

help.

Undoing the girl I labored to build,
subsuming her in a body,
a conflict.

Everyone warned her
my violence was progressive,
that she'd end up like this.

The development, the interrogated mirror
every inch, my threat
potential, our resemblance,
what I want,
whether it is to hurt you.

I do not forgive you because I do not think
we are different.

It is no special gift
                    our vague diagnostic

          lacking a stable internal sense of self

nothing to live for without ___________

          experiences every threat
          as a threat of annihilation

might be a side effect except
                    that it was there before.

The Means

KNIFE

A classic choice.
I come easily to hand. You can
almost recall inventing me,
deep in your monkey blood
how you sat pulling the edge
against stone until the blade
was born. I work for you every
day. Born as fused twins, I cut
your fabric. In the kitchen
I saw through burned cow flesh
but dream of your living hand.
You test our loyalty, make
us into safety razors and feed us
nothing but hair until you toss
us out in wadded tissue. The
parts for box cutters with their flat
edges like the tops of buildings.
I am thirsty. I am an impoverished
god. I want you to say my name.
I love the little ridges on the outside
of your body, remembrances
of where I have been. I can feel
you itch for it, showing
me where to go. Down to
bone. I want to discover you.
To make you into the truth you
are. Wet heap. Split seam.
Dead meat.

First Time

It sounds worse / than it was: He was married / mid-30s. I was fourteen. / I had no choice / dissolving into July. / Keep trying to say / what I wanted / when I did all those things / I did not want. / He had crooked front teeth / and the kind of beard that happens / from not doing anything. The car / a station wagon. Pale blue. / In the library. Afternoon. / In the car. He asked / eyes on the road / first with a euphemism and then / when I failed to understand / with rough language / pulled my head down / armrest pushed into my ribs / everything made / to this purpose. / Drove to a park I had been to / with my parents / pulled into the mouth / of a trail / had me kneel in the dirt / urgent / which I thought was sweet / grunted and put his hand / behind my head / apologized / drove me back downtown. / After he finished   / for a moment / for no reason / I could name / I thought / he was going / to kill me. /
I thought I was going to die.

Hollywood Confessions, 1996. Self-Erasure

Get it right

whatever I am

religion
the seizures

clear: end it.

cameras
forgive me

sweetheart

unhooks
my ribs from behind

pictures in which
I do not appear

sunset coaxed
from my body
tarnishing. Forced
into small wisdom

I lived in my
skin like a hell
Rich cushioned casket
of the girl I killed. Myself.

Blonde mythology

box nailed shut
My tongue
I see the rest
of the world
and I lie

in it.

The Deadgirl and I in Couples Therapy

The counselor is sweet. Mousy looking.
I can't help but think she doesn't know
what she's up against. How I keep trying
to change and not being able to. How my
baby is beyond putting in any effort.

The counselor says to make lists of what
we like about each other. Here is my list
about her:

she looks incredible in red.

she is really, really funny, without trying to be.

how glitter sticks to her skin so hard, you have to
daub it off with oil.

she looks great on film. Photographs. Home movies.

I just feel like she's known me forever.

her taste in music. I often forget to put on music, so
you understand, it's nice
to have some sweet noise in the house.

when I am really sad sometimes she'll take off her
feet and stick forks in them
and do that Chaplin routine. It is the most
adorable thing you can
imagine.

the char at the edge of the wound on her thigh. How
the fire keeps coming back.

the death, which is the secret reason
behind every thing I do. How it moves
between us like an air current
like a silk dress.

when I'm all the way inside her, how seeds of light
start to spark from her throat
and forehead.

What she likes about me:

that I am loud.
that I am mean.
that lipstick never stays on my mouth.
my bereavement.
feverbeaten.
absolute.
obelisk.
my knives.
the living. How sex builds itself
like a hive within me.
the way my hair grows in. Thick
and hideous
and more. More.

The Means

GUN

I was made for war
and game. Those were
happy years.
I was a late bloomer when
it came to girls, but once
I'd been introduced
how could I ever get enough?
Tunneled past whalebone
and crinoline, opened
a wet blooming under
their dress. Now the
ladies, they love me. They
know my names and my
aliases. I do what
your man can't. Smuggled
or paraded, stripped
and shined. Don't let the
tough-guy act fool you,
I love the ladies back.
When it seems I am just
laying heavy in your lap
I am asking for a kiss
your mouth's soft ceiling, pale,
heavy, lady's
brain up there, still
and helpless as a sleeping cat.
Bury the senseless, disposable part
of myself inside you like
a stopper. Even though

I won't care for you as much
in the morning. Even though
a kiss is never
enough.

Denied Involvement

After initially denying involvement or any cover-up in the deaths of three Afghan women during a badly bungled American Special Operations assault in February, the American-led military command in Kabul admitted late on Sunday that its forces had, in fact, killed the women during the nighttime raid… "There was evidence of tampering at the scene, walls being washed, bullets dug out of holes in the wall," the NATO official said, adding that investigators "couldn't find bullets from the wounds in the body."

–April 4, 2010, The New York Times

we forgive you because

(STONES / BURDEN / BORDER / THE WORK / OF YOUR
YOUNG LIFE / FEATHERS / OUR SURVIVING CHILDREN)

we don't forgive you

(ONLY YOU SURVIVED / SOLDIERS / THE COMPOUND /
DEAFENED / SO THE ONLY WAY ANYONE WILL KNOW IS
IF YOU TELL IT)

when you dug the bullets out of the wounds

(YOUR EYES / BLUE BLUE BLUE BLUE / A TIDE / WINGS
STUCK TOGETHER / THE RADIANT CROWN / THE NAME
OF THE BEAST / THAT WILL BEAR US TO SAFETY / THE
NAME OF THE CREATURE / THAT WILL DIG OUR BONES UP)

used alcohol, inexplicably, to clean us

(WHEN WE COME FOR YOUR / SONS / WET EARTH
CAKED ON OUR ROBES / WHEN WE COME / FOR YOUR
DAUGHTERS / YOUR WIVES / TO SHOW THEM / WHAT

YOU HAVE / DONE TO WOMEN / THERE IS NO TEMPLE YOU CAN BUILD WITHOUT / US UNDERNEATH IT)

we forgive you because it is endearing. you seemed not to know how it worked

(YOU DID NOT WILL US TO / BE / HERE THE SOOT IN OUR HAIR / DID NOT PRY YOUR EYES OPEN / THINKING THE WOMAN / YOUR ENEMY / WE KNOW / YOU DID NOT INVENT THIS / DID NOT BLOODHOUND US OUT OF DREAMS OF YOUR MOTHERS / DO NOT SEE US CROUCHED / IN THE DARK CORNERS / OF THE DAUGHTERS YOU WILL / OR WILL NOT HAVE / AFTER YOU DUG THE BULLET OUT / A DEEP BUT EMPTY GOUGE)

like you wanted to unkill us.

United States Army Private First Class LaVena Johnson to Sarah Palin

Dear Sarah
        from the moment I saw you
beatific, anointed in news-ticker light
I knew you were meant for me
        that you would change my life
we are so alike
        I don't just mean the woman thing

your small town, a place
where nothing bad could happen
        photographs of you beside your husband
halos of animal fur around your pink faces

what a terror for you to be there, Sarah
under the midnight sun
to know your body
would make you a meal in times of famine
thighs rendered for lard   hair stuffed in
to soften a sawdust mattress
I see you running   desperation
to feel yourself God's chosen daughter
decided all the other lives were second
inferred sanctity into the function of ovaries
God's will in the dropping of dirty bombs

If you were not you
if you were some housewife
stranded in middle America
you would be so forgivable
but you are you—

you cunning pillowlips
you are the chosen

So when you said, in Wasilla
    that rape survivors
should pay for their own forensic tests
I knew what had happened
that you had passed
through the curtain
into a place where women
    are not women.
Where women do not live

now you're there you think
the power they gave you will protect you
like moss green poplin
and brass buttons would protect me
they would have to admit I was human
if I showed that love of country

You know what they did Sarah—
the contractors in our own employ
    abrasions   loose teeth   burns on my hands
the acid   they poured into me   to burn out
their DNA   the hole
they put in my head
could not have been made
by my shooting hand
and they told my mother it was a suicide

the molecules of my last breath
spread out over the desert

glintingsugary sand in the dawning light—
it looked like snow

if there is a god like you believe in God, Sarah
He keeps me here
waiting for you
my mother's anguish twisting me four legged—
I scan the horizon
          my time will come

you will fall from your helicopter
your rifle will kick and jam
I will feel your throat pulse
against the gray fur of my jaws

and you will know me   Sarah
flesh of your flesh

this is oddly
politically sincere
which is a little
refreshing at this
point

The Parts of Her They Kept

After her death in 1815, parts of Saartjie "Little Sarah" Baartman's corpse were kept in a museum in France, until 2002 when Nelson Mandela's 1994 request that her remains be returned to South Africa was finally honored. In life, Sarah was sold into slavery a number of times, forced to perform in exhibitions, human zoos, under the name The Hottentot Venus.

I. Brain

They took it out looking for difference,
I am sure. Some touching deficiency.
So they pried it free, pink washing
severed into cerebral fluid, soft gray-white
ridges of a sad organ. Imagine their
delight. Careful smiles behind
surgical masks at whatever
had killed me (wrote down *smallpox*,
but called *Syphilis* to each other
across the morgue.)
They held it a moment in their hands,
pale meat where everything had been recorded.
Every curious pink prodding finger
every hurled head
of rotting lettuce,
every dawning recognition in blue-white
eyes as they heaved into me—terror of what
might be human in the dark
orbs of my form. If it were true,
if I were a woman
what monsters that made them.

II. Skeleton

Because they could not remove
and display my blackness
on its own, they did the next best thing.
Stripped the flesh with knives
then boiled the bones clean.
Wrote out small placards
to accompany it.
my bones—blood factories.
Busy cities spitting red
from indestructible hearts.
You cannot imagine,
from the pale church they tried to build of me,
what fluid life I constantly mined from
my essential hardness.

III.

I would like, for a moment, to talk only
to the white girls. Thin volumes of theory
protesting the unrealistic beauty standard.
Engineers of ad campaigns
who only let the thinnest, whitest-looking
Black girl in. Let me tell you a story.

When I was alive I would not let them
display the core of the exotica,
extra inch of rippling labia
proof that my animal sex
was dripping out of me,
reaching to devour.

They never marched me out
into the bright tent
with it showing
not even when white men fucked me
for money in private.

So when I died
what do you think they did?
Right.
Preserved it. Made plaster casts
from the original. Stuck it to a velvet
bed with long brass pins
and put it in the Musée under glass.
Understand, when a black woman
is paraded as a fuck-beast
it is only mostly because of her race.
Understand that what
you clasp between your pale thighs
is reason enough to exhibit you.
They've refrained
because they know your father
because their son
might want to marry you one day.

Wound Seduction Manual

FOUND TEXT COLLAGE

I'm sure you've seen guys who find it
incredibly easy to chat up girls
they make it look so easy assessing the
vulvo-vaginal structures

this was the main reason for us to develop
a new technique which mostly satisfies

when he introduces himself for instance
he'll shake hands but let his hand linger
a second longer than you might expect
allowing infection to invade the bloodstream (sepsis)

you can see the process starting immediately
a saline-moistened dressing
is allowed to dry and
adhere then pulled off without hesitation
the dressing can stick to living tissue as well
to get her all fluttery-eyed and laughing
and opening up to you

a wound cannot be properly evaluated
until the dead tissue
or foreign matter is removed
this is a delight to watch.
assessing physical factors
that limit vaginal dimension
he never throws himself at women
not every wound requires intervention

sometimes it is necessary to leave some dead tissue
different skin (penile scrotal abdominal
labial vaginal flaps etc.) artery
nerves or shyness I suppose when your mind goes blank
and you can't think of anything interesting

waiting too long exact time depending
on individual physiology
leads to difficulty restarting dilation

It doesn't matter whether you want to seduce
every second woman who comes along
or just make that one special girl
fall in love with you
the key is keeping the wound moist
it is more selective
than any other method
but it also takes the longest to work

it can also be used successfully in children

tightening the surrounding soft tissues
she lowered her eyes submissively
and began a pharmaceutical version
of the body's processes
I doubt that she was at all aware
of what she was doing

although serious complications
were reported in the past
new techniques
seem to be safe in experienced hands.

True Hollywood Confessions of 1944

My secretary found me
but she knew
dead actresses belong to everyone,
the way my life did.
The screen behind
my face rolling back and away
from the leading man.

I set the scene, satin nightgown,
rose petal strewn bed,
evening slippers tufted with marabou.
I didn't know what the pills would do

exactly, other than kill me.
Didn't know about the nausea,
the last hour heaving on the bathroom tiles
toilet water slicking my hair
into my face like a raven's wing.

I had hoped for more
romance, but afterwards
I was as dead as I could want.
Editors from those trashy papers
loved my early work—the silents
where I learned to glow and faint.

They knew that I was pregnant,
blood collecting purple-black under
my hip, tried to recast me, a cautionary tale

blamed the boy who would not marry me
or else, my hot-blooming, exotic mouth
foaming chemistry in my pretty skull.

I was born, covered
in silty mother-water
to a failed opera singer
who only hoped
I would be worth her time.

For all the articles about my
vanity, my wasted talent
I know that this is not only my story.
Fancy-dress general of this secret army.

You're on my side. You hope
that young man remembered me
the rest of his life. My legion
lies awake, imagining
their own death
in slow motion, complete
with epilogue; how peaceful
the casket. How sorry
we will make everyone.

Mae, Fatale

Despite how dull and cold the light,
you glowed with life, luster of
your radiant hair brushed out across
pale sloping shoulders—what you must have been like.

You glowed with life. Luster of
the silk gleams, your beloved shape,
pale sloping shoulders. What you must have been like
to hold. What mad scientist's conjuring—

the silk's gleam, your beloved shape.
The hourglass assembled of growl and camerawork
to hold what? Mad scientist conjuring
sand falling into your bedroom slippers,

the hourglass. Assembled of growl and camerawork
as you turned sex into a dress with no seam,
sand falling into your bedroom slippers
Men collapsing into you like houses of cards

as you turned sex into a dress with no seam,
a joke you were forever getting or making.
Men collapsing against you like houses of cards
lowing for their own slaughter, to become

a joke you were always getting or making.
They remember you like parishioners.
Lowing for their own slaughter, to become
The fur around your plunging neckline

They remember you like parishioners,
your radiant hair brushed out across
the fur around your plunging neckline
despite how dull and cold, the light.

The Ghost in My Mind's Small Reach Says

our suffering is the largest one,
and it's impolite
to argue. She says, forget it,

cameraphone become an
amateur snuff film, forget,
the subway platform
facedown. The ghost

is my only hope for glory
she wants to tell our story
she wants it to be the one
that's most important.

The ghost says the dead
don't care for justice,
feathers springing
from her plucked-out eyes.
I tell her she only thinks that
because she's white.

How to Pull Romona Moore Out of Your Hat

I have done everything you've asked me to do. I've looked everywhere. I've talked to everyone you wanted me to. I can't find her. I can't find your daughter. She doesn't want to be found. I can't find her. I'm not a magician. I cannot pull her out of my hat.

–Detective Wayne Carey to Elle Carmichael, Romona Moore's mother

Start by putting things into the hat.
An hourglass chasing sandy minutes
backward. The graduation photograph—
her thick grin under the white mortarboard.
Put Remsen Avenue in the hat.
Give the fathers back to the boys.
Suck the blood up from the streets.
Find a police officer with a teenage daughter
and have them crawl inside.

This must not be in the hat: Scissors
Shoelaces. Tire irons. Tumors
with teeth the city calls *men*.

Remember what you are up against.
What you are trying to undo. Skull fracture
cut webbing between her fingers
pink gummed surface of the
cigarette burns. How hard it is
to break a young woman's hip.

Now pull from the hat
the ninety-six hours
covered in duct tape,
in broken glass.

The black silk draping
her mother's memory of everything
she saw for months
powdered Xanax, a crumb trail
leading her back to the world of living.

Pull out the long ribbon of paper
from the court typist's machine
its punched staccato of black girls
ghosted off Flatbush.
No Ophelia. No trawling the river.
No high, bright pyre. The ditch.
The dark and no news story.

At last, pull her slowly
from the satin mouth.

And you think it works that way—
          if she wanted to be found
Romona's thorax would split
and fill the room with light.
skin cells radiating free
of the carpet fibers
fluid searing itself off
of their hands and penises
until she was never theirs, never
kept under a tarp in the basement.
Transformed into a
light they cannot hold
in their minds without
maddening pain.

I do not see why that is so difficult,
Officer. They should have taught you
this at the academy. You should
have learned by now.

C _ _ _ G _ _ _ _ T

HIS SUICIDE

You paste pictures of the girl
who broke off your engagement
write her pet name in blood
on the walls of your cell.

We are an odd couple
yet we have everything in common
now that you have killed yourself.

Once, asleep
I saw your wedding night.
Peeled back the white satin
where she was sealed up
like melted wax against you.
So you took a scalpel
and tried to correct it,
diagrams in your textbook
reconstructive
        a good attempt
that word that at first you thought
        meant *the removal of the bride.*

Her scream inside
her sealed-shut mouth
but by then
you could not stop it

        seconds burying themselves
like blades
in the thing you had hoped
to love.

Serial

When your heart finally opened, burst,
A carburetor you could not repair—
the girls escaped in a shower of rust,

stumbling. Daylight blinded them at first.
Iron fastenings flaking into the air.
When you finally opened, burst,

the horizon stretched, an opening fist,
the world outside you before them, bared.
The girls escaped in a shower of rust

and would not come back, for pity or for lust.
You thought, unfair.
When your heart finally opened. Burst

everything that had been yours. You must
have been amazed they left your lair,
the girls. Escaped in a shower of rust.

That's why you'd locked them up, you couldn't trust
them. They left you here, without a prayer.
Your heart. Final. Opened. Burst.
The girls escaped in a shower of rust.

Their Father Is Sleeping on the Couch

and wakes up with blood on his face.
Two men drag him into his basement
he is tied hand and foot.
One of the men takes the wife
to the bank to make a withdrawal.
The other man stays behind
to violate the children.
The children are girls
eleven and seventeen.
The wife withdraws the money,
$15,000, from a teller.
Gets back in the car.
When she gets home, they rape her
and strangle her until she is dead.
One of them has brought
some kerosene. They tie the girls
to their beds
and pour it over them.
The father hears them say
This will all be over in a couple of minutes
and believes that it means
he is about to be shot.
While the men are busy
the father breaks away
bashes through the cellar door
rolls into the neighbor's yard.
The police come.
The girls have died of smoke inhalation.
They catch the men. So.
Here are our options.
          No god or a god
who let this happen.

Here is our cast of characters.
The people who we might be:
The woman
who thinks that doing
what she is told
must be enough to save them.

The two caught men.

The father
who survives.

The girls
who are where the fire starts.

Dozens

After Angel Nafis after Terrance Hayes after Dr. Seuss

Deadgirl worth the cover / Deadgirl what you paid to see / Deadgirl howling in the sky / Deadgirl house is every house / Deadgirl recipe: girl, add almost anything / Deadgirl sandwiched between cellophane sheets / Deadgirl sandwiched between sports and local / Deadgirl your misspeech at the party / Deadgirl longing bastion / Deadgirl packed close as pomegranate seed / Deadgirl smokestack / Deadgirl crosswalk / Deadgirl you see again in the dream of the field / Deadgirl you see again in the dream of the factory / Deadgirl you see again in the dream of the ocean / Deadgirl on the billboard / Deadgirl quietly / Deadgirl sensitive about her appearance / Deadgirl marionette / Deadgirl video cassette / Deadgirl irony of the receptacle / Deadgirl donated to science / Deadgirl bad at staying buried / Deadgirl working on an awareness campaign / Deadgirl un-function / Deadgirl un-decide / Deadgirl dissolve before your eyes / Deadgirl dead center / Deadgirl dead end / Deadgirl deadlock / Deadgirl dead ass / Deadgirl discoball / Deadgirl shroud harpy / Deadgirl ankles thin as money / Deadgirl formaldehyde mix in the honey / Deadgirl hosed off the sidewalk / Deadgirl heavy as a Cadillac / Deadgirl inanimate intimate / Deadgirl plummeting through the cloud / Deadgirl knocking at your chest like a door / Deadgirl inside already / Deadgirl make herself at home / Deadgirl wearing your old housedress / Deadgirl humming a song you hate / Deadgirl laughing you out of church / Deadgirl laughing church out of you / Deadgirl shows up all dovewing and scimitar / Deadgirl says it's all in your head / Deadgirl's been watching you die since sunrise was a new idea / Deadgirl knows you won't meet her eye / Deadgirl says how special you're not / Deadgirl mistook you for her twin / Deadgirl arriving / Deadgirl / departing / Dead / girl who I've / always been

Meeting the Father-in-Law

God shows up at my apartment with a list
of edicts against closeness
between the living
and the dead.

I say *I know it's unorthodox*
but I'm not hurting anyone.

He sighs. Pushes his hat brim back.
Says *I'm sorry this is how*
you have to find out.
I look around the room
for something of hers.
Reassurance. Her boots
on the floor where she always
left them. But there's nothing.
Little streamers of opalescent smoke
rising off the floorboards.
What is this? I say
Where has she gone, anyhow?

He says *I wish she'd told you*
herself. This is embarrassing.

I say *Did you do this?*
Take her away?
Because I will ghost myself.
You think I won't? I'll follow her.

He says *Listen.*
She is not in love with you.

I say *We had an*
understanding. I don't mind
being second best.

He says *If you had an understanding,*
why am I here? You were not
second. You were not on the list.
You're not the kind of thing she likes.
Look at yourself.
Look at this place.
You think you could
take care of her?

His shoulder dips back
    I think
        Let him try it—
        let him try to hit me

He shrugs his jacket back on, turns,
and God leaves my house.
The door clicks shut behind him.

C _ A _ G _ L _ _ T

ARRAIGNMENT

We can all see you suffering
no doctor for

the red snake circling your gut
no one to tell you

how common your mistake
revulsion a hair's breadth

beyond desire
its outline visible through the skin

Philip, you were mostly wrong
but not all wrong.

Right about the terror,
how it makes you cry like a child.

But it leaves you so
un-murdered. So alive.

After She Left

Despite our attempts to mutilate them
the dead stay perfect. Look at her go.
Look at that ass

still, as
memory licks her edges
like a blind dog.

Life, a small hurricane of
interferences with grief.
There's nowhere else.

Not in her grave
where she will not have you.
Not in her shut mouth which is no

longer hers. Not in the clear
immutable joy of the gone days
when she said she wanted to see you.

But here. In your house
of paste and wax. Alongside all
these men looking at their watches

a concert hall whose orchestra
suddenly quiets. The floor, like
a glacier, cracks and shifts.

The Mother-in-Law

Tonight I sleep with silence my impossible white wife
–Yusef Komunyakaa

My wedding negligee spun
from blood and rope, proof
you can bleach anything to silk,
my ancestors, a fury of absence, inbred Olympus,
crowned with spikes of mountain laurel.

You know what I'll do to our children
and it hounds you from our bed,
how I'd not teach them to apologize
or wield a hammer. The endless retouching
of my old photographs, brushing
the stretchmark invisible,
belly torn open revealing bread

my beauty an icesheet sloughing
off, my beauty the milk occlusion growing over
your eyes, my beauty your pain and its erasure,
the color of surrender and of empire.
The graces, a series of traipsing women
who all resemble me,
sewn into the spines
of each volume in your library.

The baby inside me flicks open a safety pin
and swallows it. I run out of inventions
to hurt you. Pinning badges to my eyes.
A whir of spokes, air blurred silver
with drones. I'm here so you'll always

have something to kill for. Bleach
on the tile, bleach flushed into
the womb, bleach covered with vanilla,
fiberglass, silicone, promise of a bloodless coup.
Didn't I teach you
to undance to every song?

The Means

NOOSE

I could arrive from anywhere. Any scarf,
any stocking. An old belt. Shoelaces.
even when the knives and pills and
nasty things are taken cautiously out
you have not gotten rid of me. I hide.
I transform. I know the glory of the
breath, ridged tunnel of its passage
small throbbing lines of fluid along
the sides of the neck. The muscles'
twitch and slacken, vision gone dark
then fireworked with stars. Some of them
come to me in search of orgasm, or else
they are thinking of wild west outlaws:
gallows for everyone to see their tough
wronged glory. But when my own girls come,
they come to die. To be held in the dark
forever, heavily, no more breath or choices
they freshen the water in the dog's bowl,
pick an hour of the day they have all to
themselves, and they fashion me, loop
and hitch of the long fabric. They know
the way the body will shed its waste
how the face will twist, contort, they
know they will not be pretty. But I see
in them that devotion. I hold them in a slow
twirl. My newfound brides. Daughters
of air.

Debridement

Removal of damaged tissue from a wound
–Earliest use 1839, from the French, débridement, lit. "an unbridling."

When its own rot prevents it
from healing, holds it open
a wetness devouring itself,
the task is to coax the wound,
stab the edge raw enough
to discover a desire to grow
back.

The body trying to seal up
cannot stop weeping
cannot push the infection out
too generous a host to its injury.

At the beginning of the story
I found a girl inside my wound,
tried to remove her.
I could not. Now every allegiance
to this (feminine flesh) splits
raw across my face.

And if removing
what kept your wound open
means you have lost
your lover, what then?
If the wound
is your only family resemblance
and without it you wander
a bastard among your kind.

Wound Seduction Manual

FOUND TEXT COLLAGE

With this book, you'll have the confidence
and charm to walk up to any girl anywhere
and construct the functional
and cosmetically acceptable penis.

Normal penis has unique characteristics:
He is very quick to pick up on what women say to him.
an exquisite way of identifying
the words that are important
to a woman *Competent* *Hairless*
Satisfactory appearance
feeding them back to her in his conversation

When he walks into a room,
their eyes seem to fall upon him immediately.
He has a certain way of positioning himself
inserting a gloved finger
to estimate depth and evaluate risk.

As he talks with her he'll start
by looking into her eyes then allow his gaze
to momentarily follow the line of
the urethral stent
using forceps to grip the dead tissue
then linger for a split-second on her breasts
before coming back to look closely
into her donor site defect again.

At the same time, he does all of this
playfully and with a sense of fun—

incision—the pubic area
excise a tunnel.

You're going to learn all their best secrets—
the location of the wound in the body,
the type of pain management to be used,
the signals that tell you
she wants to take things further.
        How long will it take?
                How much will it hurt?
Post operative outcome is variable,
usually allows for coitus although
full sensation might not be present

And when the time is right, you'll know
how to pop the question in a way
that makes it difficult
        for her to say *No.*

The Means

PILLS

We are the cure for that.
We are the medicine.
We sing you inside out, scatter
our powder from shoulder
to ovary. We open within
you like storms. If your
life were perfect, you
would not even have
us around the house
and we know that.
We're the ugly suitor—
we hate you. Swing ourselves
like wrecking balls down
your throat. Before
there was some romance
to it, a poison draught from
the apothecary. These
days we all do double duty
as the agents of wakefulness
or sleep, encouragers
of the blood, pain's small
adversaries sent in legions.
This way, everyone always
half-wonders if it was an
accident. Maybe you thought
you were having a party.
Maybe you thought someone
would come home in time to
pump your pretty stomach.
You sick girl. I've got your

number. Talked sweet to you
for a long time before the
relationship went south.
Remember what we used
to have? The body you
wanted? The anesthetic?
The sweet, uninterrupted
dreams? We are the remedy.
We're taking you home.

Aubade for Venus Xtravaganza

I am trying to fall asleep without masturbating
again and the sun is coming up. Fuck.
I turn my face farther into the cushioned
wreck. My pillow smells like
my hair oil and my drool and no one else.

You said you wished you were
white and rich. That white girls always
get what they want.
If it were that year ('87?
'89?) I could find you
somewhere. I could buy

you. Your hands like birds,
your unimaginable penis.
Watch you try to pull back
from it, strain, the soft puddle
a dawn cloud streaking your chest.
Bleached gold scrim
of your showgirl hair.

You would not love me. I would write
some stupid poem about the crest of your hip
like a wave. Embittered,
the flowers hot-glued to the bodice
of the dress that you street-walked in.

Painted cheekbones
tan gloss smeared on your
split peach mouth, your tongue
a stinger, sucking sugar from bruised
fruit. I would torture myself.

All the arms you'd been in
that were not mine.
Dawn would break like this, like now,

I'd be alone in bed. I hate that sex does not
Matter. Crying
like a teenage girl.

This should not be
what I say to you.
I should talk
about your bravery

how you saw it
coming, the woman that you would be
and did not run,
but opened your skinny arms

and walked toward her across
the dawn paling sand,

metamorphosis I've evaded
all my life
where you end up a woman.
The cost you paid,
          Fine. I'll hustle.
My parents' names
a scar housing a small ache. I'll walk
into the female danger
and deeper
and farther. I'll be the girl
          even though

you must have known—
daylight breaking
            completely, now—
            you must have known
            the girl is dead.

When They Come for Your Body the Last Time

they are wearing dark blue.
You are naked in the road. Someone
called it in from a payphone.
Far away, a tree burns red with fruit.
The things you wish you'd told your
mother. The tissue, at first
pounded into a new tenderness
then, as the pump stopped and you
lost your heat, hardened.
Tough ridge of your shoulder
where it pressed against the road.
Newscasters swarm over
the details, parceling you out
like filets wrapped in butcher paper.
And the next one, already out there.
Metal hearts hanging from her ears.
For a moment, as you're leaving
you can see her, her warm skin
like sugar-butter. Awaiting
his handprint. The cold. The basement.
You try to tell her something, a
whisper, unease. You try to fuse the
pearl of your skull back together,
close your legs. Turn the pages
of her book in an empty room
to reveal something that could be
taken as a warning.
Even this, you are denied.

First Time

Walking from my house
to the coffeeshop I thought
was the coolest place on earth,
I was wearing combat
boots and a black party dress.
I was wearing a dog collar
and underpants that I thought were sexy
because they were velvety in the front
and sheer in their generous
grandmotherly backside.
He was an older man

in a car. He saw me and pulled
into a parking lot. He was graying,
or the car was gray, or it was
white and dirty. He rolled down
the window. Idling,
his hands where I could see them
on the wheel, the car's ashtray
sifting up pale flakes.

He asked if I was a dominatrix.
I said I had been but
my boyfriend made me stop.
I was fifteen. I lied as easy as breath.
I had never been made
to stop doing anything. My boyfriend
was 23, the author of every
thought in my head.

The man in the car asked
if he could buy my underwear.

I tried to take them off
but he said *No, not out there*
opened the passenger door,
burst capillaries
on the rubble of his cheeks.
I got in. Pulled the panties
over my boots, the warm,
crumpled money in my hand, fast.
He said   *Sorry, sorry,*
popped the car door

beige plush of the seat
loosing its grip on my thighs.
I had always imagined

my worth to be that. Now I was
right. My boyfriend took it as a compliment
to his own good taste,

laughed about it. For years
I did not think
            it was the beginning.

C R A _ G S L _ S T

BEFORE THEY CATCH YOU

I walked by the hotel
where you had done it.
The windows' champagne gleam
clientele in their evening casual.
The glass membrane
keeping out the bums
who sleep in Back Bay
under church blankets
the color of lint.
You were here
striding through
the revolving door
nodding to the valet.
Your sandy clean-cut hair
on the surveillance tape.

If we do not know each other
it is an accident.
Walking through the clear
New England evening
I wonder what you're doing.
Probably eating.

They called it a murder in the paper,
as though all you did to the call girl
was shoot her in the chest.
As though your dick
never throbbed against your thigh
when you read the ad.
The tabloid headlines churn

out dead hooker puns.
Do you think you are right?

Let me tell you who is right:
the lank-haired head found in the dumpster
and the girlchild naked in the riverbed
and the pregnant waddler strangled
in the Applebee's parking lot
and every dead call girl, every one
staring back from the inside
of the hot final moment
hollow and flooded
with light—they knew

and the injustice was
the almost-anything
they would have done for you
how they moved toward you
already half-slaughtered in the sheets.
They saw your eyes—
only special
in that you'd be the last

they knew.
Someone had hurt you
and they were paying for it.

*

ARREST

The first picture they release,
Philip, you are at party or graduation
white oxford shirt open
at your throat, your head tilts back
laughing: it could be the face
from a roman coin.
Your fiancée, chestnut hair cascading
says she loves you, reads
her prepared statement, will   not
come out of the house.

Some other girl you forced
into a kiss one boozy night
spills it to the evening news.
The anchor can think of nothing
to say except how much
like other college kids you are.
The victim's panties
are found in your apartment.
They won't stop taking
your future wife's picture,
telephoto prying at
her living room window
suddenly permeable as skin.

Villanelle Self-Erasure

his body
he can't unthrone

What you learn first

her fresh-bit lip
his property

Salt *apology*
you learn

his father's hands sprout from his wrists

keening

In dreams, he's bought her crematory urn.

What you learn first, you never unlearn.

When the Deadgirl Came Back To Me

I did not expect it. I had spent years
in the village of wool and bone
forgetting the blood was ever
anyone's but mine. You came over
the hill, and the pigs began to rut
in the mud, their pink-white bellies
streaked with it. Your sleeve tore
on the nail in the gate, and you cried.
You apologized for the time,
how it fell like smoke through
the still air around us. The headstones
growing from your footprints. Apologized for how
you were dressed, your skirt made of scissors
announcing your arrival like a small
tin chime. You said you were ready
now. And all the buildings
made of toothpicks and yarn fell to the ground.
The wedding band I'd worn
caught fire like it was made of string.
And my blood rioted for your blood
which was still. The clouded blue
of your nearly-lost eye.

The Deadgirl Takes Control

She says I should at least let her try it.
That I never let her express herself.
So I say *Fine, if it's important. If you*
want, you can wear one of my outfits.
She does. Straps me to the bed with my
mouth taped up. She says *How do I look?*
Says *Sure, for you it's a fun change of pace.*
but for me it's like that all the time.

*

Her breasts, through the leather
press into my stomach.
She says *You've been wrong*
the whole time. *It hurts, being dead.*
I think, she's trying to get me to cry,
that's all. She doesn't mean it.
Hold me, she laughs
when my wrists move against the straps.
She uses drams of strange drugs,
stones wrapped in silk, swung around
like flails. She knows this because she endured it
and did not, exactly, survive.

*

She asks what I could not live without
presses her fingertips against my eyes
then closes my ears
with the heels of her hands.
What could you not live without,
really? Light cracking

between her vertebra, ghost sound
pouring through her teeth.

*

She:

Remember when I left you
the first time
and took with me the kiss
to which you swore
your breath was married
and your traitorous lungs
kept heaving and surviving it
kept pulling you farther out
from the land of the dead?
The tiniest, most senseless
things will deprive you.
A cylinder of lead the size of your fingertip
An odd clot of cells. A man
who loved you in the only way available
to him.
A chicken bone you did not expect.

A moment's panic, breathing in instead of out.

*

She:

No. You're not so smart,
you can't just keep avoiding me.
You think you're such hot shit
not holding my hand
in public.

*

She blindfolds me and is quiet for a long

time:

You're using me so you won't have to deal
with the terror of your own empty life.

*

The deadgirl knows my limit
better than I do.
The veins flickering through the back of her hand.

You idiot. You think
you've only written this.

Uterine

Laboring through her bloody tenure
flanked by a hormonal retinue
she's center stage, the muscular tureen
that keeps me from my maleness, from neuter.
Her ermine riffling vainly, the dated tune
she hums to her contentment. Monthly ruin
of my skin, my neurochemistry. Discrete unit
of my earthly worth. How to inure
poor brainy against her onslaught? How reunite
the cave-dwelling beast with the sharp tine
of my human purpose, if she is what's true?

First Time

I drank a lot of something.
It was his. It was not
what I wanted
but I thought this was how it
was done. I was 16. I did not
want to die, but
we had fought, and
he said he was serious. That
he was leaving. I stayed up
late. I wrote some letters.
I intended to die but
what I wanted was
                                        Long airborne
shapes of his boy's body.
I intended for him
to find me. The cuts on my wrists
were deep but not long. That
was my mistake. I dressed up
the way he liked me to, and got
in the bathtub to wait. Warm
water. I don't know where
I got my information. He
found me. Pulled me up from
the tub, the water barely pink.
His shut lips. For a few days, every-
thing was fine. His small red car
with its manual shift. My head
sleepy in his lap. His fine-boned
face. Love. Like a jaw wired shut.

The Frontier

purple flowers blind turn toward the sun.
Rust-colored streaks of earth
between knots of groundcover.
The sky a blue. The world
stares back at you.
I am in the field watching

blossoms rustle in the wind
the woman is in the field watching
I can be nowhere nothing else.
The woman wringing her hands.

Wind moving through the subway
rustling her hair like a flower.
His leather gloves, her rustled breast,
the wind moving through it.

The woman in the field dreams of children.
The field weeps, cricket, songbird, wet
leaf unfolding. The car alarms harrowing my block.

She lived in a wooden house,
a pass between the mountains.
Her people left, or died.
The man carried a stick
as he was walking a long distance.

A wet day in spring.
His old leather coat.
No one to dig a hole or wear black lace.
Left above ground
for the wind to rustle in, like a flower, her purple dress,

red streaked through it.
This was before there were newspapers.

Her body left in the open
air inside my body. This story tells itself
no matter how few remain—

when I have to play the woman's corpse
and also the highwayman.
Even when no one
peers through the buds
of new growth
to drool at the crime.

Take the world away from me,
pin my arms in a whitewashed cell
and I will still know
that it happened,
that it's happening.

Acknowledgements

Ocean Vuong, kindest, patientest, and most brilliant of editors, helped me immeasurably in developing this book. I cannot possibly thank him enough.

This book also wants to declare its allegiance to some other books, a sort of infentessimal sub-genre: *Last Seen* by Jaqueline Jones LaMon, *Patient.* by Bettina Judd, *Kissing Dead Girls* by Daphne Gottlieb, and Patricia Smith's forthcoming collection all feel integral to this work.

I am very thankful for the support and friendship of Sasha Warner-Berry, Tara Hardy, John Paul Davis, the Kagan-Trenchards, and my parents, as well as the kind attentions of Jane Ormerod, Thomas Fucaloro, and David Lawton at great weather for MEDIA who have made this shockingly painless.

About the Author

Corrina Bain is a gender non-conforming writer, performer, teaching artist, and a former member and coach of multiple national-level poetry slam teams. His writing has appeared in anthologies and journals such as *Muzzle Magazine*, *PANK*, *A Face to Meet the Faces*, and the Everyman's Library collection *Villanelles*. Corrina's work engages the nuances of the body as a source of identity, pleasure, betrayal, and shame. While deeply rooted in the personal and specific, his vision extends to encompass history, mythology, and politics. No injustice, hypocrisy, or human weakness escapes this poet's gaze, especially his own. Searching beyond violence, he suggests there is power in trusting the body's wisdom, in witnessing suffering, and in speaking what you do not dare to say. Currently, Corrina lives in Brooklyn where he practices roundhouse kicks, twerking, and emergency psychiatric counseling.

about great weather for MEDIA

Founded in January 2012, great weather for MEDIA focuses on the unpredictable, the fearless, the bright, the dark, and the innovative...

We are based in New York City and showcase both national and international writers. As well as publishing the highest quality poetry and prose, we organize numerous readings, performances, and music and art events in New York City, across the United States, and beyond.

Be sure to visit our website for details of our weekly open mic, upcoming publications, events, and how to submit work to our next anthology.

Website: www.greatweatherformedia.com

Email: editors@greatweatherformedia.com

Twitter: @greatweatherfor

Facebook: www.facebook.com/great.weather

Instagram: greatweatherformedia

great weather for MEDIA Titles

ANTHOLOGIES

Before Passing (Published Summer 2015)

I Let Go of the Stars in My Hand

The Understanding between Foxes and Light

It's Animal but Merciful

COLLECTIONS

Debridement - Corrina Bain

meant to wake up feeling - Aimee Herman

Retrograde - Puma Perl

www.greatweatherformedia.com

CPSIA information can be obtained at www.ICGtesting.com
Printed in the USA
BVOW03s1543060415

394729BV00001B/1/P